CRAIG PETERSON
For the past seven years Craig Peterson has been a
scriptwriter for top cartoonists. His work has been published
in magazines, books, and newspapers. He is also a skier –
downhill and cross-country, and has worked in the ski
business for three years, first as a ski technician and
later as a shop manager.

JERRY EMERSON
Jerry Emerson is a self-taught freelance cartoonist. His
cartoons have appeared in major magazines and trade journals
including *Saturday Evening Post,* and the *Reader's Digest.*
All of the cartoons appearing here are original and have
been prepared especially for this book.

First published October 1981 by Exley Publications Ltd,
16 Chalk Hill, Watford, Herts WD1 4BN.
ISBN 0 905521 59 5
First printing October 1981
Second printing August 1982
Third printing December 1983
Fourth printing August 1985
Fifth printing September 1986
Sixth printing June 1987

Copyright © 1980 by Stone Wall Press, Inc.
Made and printed in Great Britain by
The Guernsey Press Co. Ltd., Guernsey, Channel Islands.

the CRAZY world of SKIING

by Craig Peterson
Cartoons by
Jerry Emerson

⧉EXLEY

"My ski instructor doesn't understand me."

"You lack self-confidence Miriam—that shows good sense!"

*"Basically, my strategy will be to try and make the other racers
helpless with laughter."*

"Don't pay any attention to me – I'm still learning!"

"We came to __ski__—remember?!"

"It's more than I ever dared hope for!"

Cross Country Survival Tip Number 7
When touring the back country, remember the natural environment offers
many sources of nutrition for the resourceful.

"Pretend you're James Bond."

EASY THREE STEP SKI LESSON   Step Number 1

STANDING

RIDING

SKIING

"No, Missy. Jack and Jill didn't use the chairlift to get up the hill."

"No, we don't happen to have an opening for a ski bum."

"David, do you believe in omens?"

"Now what?"

Ski Safety Tip Number 33
Do not move an injured skier.

"To tell you the truth, it's the only stunt he knows."

GREAT MOMENTS IN SKIING

With the advanced technology of snow making, skiing is now possible in Egypt.

"Don't move—I want to forget you exactly as you are."

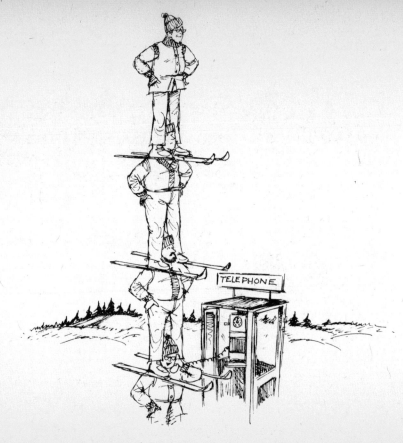

"Hello, Guinness Book of World Records . . . ?"

Cross Country Survival Tip Number 11
If a skier becomes extremely tired or exhausted on the trail,
he should find a comfortable place to rest.

*"Just teach me how to ski –
I already know how to wrestle."*

"When the newness wears off, can you store them in the basement?"

"Here comes a troublemaker."

"Watch out for __moguls__!"

*"Remember, Charlie—
our marriage counsellor says <u>I</u> should <u>lead</u> half the time!"*

CORRECT INCORRECT

Ski Safety Tip Number 24
When crossing in front of any skier, always assume his ability to be minimal.

"Don't blame yourself, Mr. Jensen. I'm probably doing something wrong."

"*I'm a beginning, advanced, novice, intermediate.
What equipment do you recommend?*"

"It's my own plan for safer skiing!"

Ski Safety Tip Number 30
To reduce risk, always
limber up your muscles before skiing.

"Comfy?"

"The guru's out skiing in Zurich . . . I'm his guest host."

"Dear, have you seen my iron?"

"No, ma'am—we don't have any skis with airbags."

"Look! Civilization!"

Ski Safety Tip Number 29
Always be prepared for the unexpected.

"All right, Murray! Who's Gloria?"

"Says our skis are in Hawaii."

"Hi? neighbour—could I borrow a cup of hot wax?"

Cross Country Survival Tip Number 13
Take special care when crossing fences.

"These books can be __purchased__ you know!"

Cross Country Survival Tip Number 8
Certain skis should be cooled before going skiing.

"It's really too bad. Before he lost his nerve, he was your complete jumper."

"The kids are just wild about our new winter home."

"My legs are being recalled for a possible steering defect."

Ski Safety Tip Number 27
Skiers should keep off closed trails and posted areas.

"I'd sell you a ticket to Paris, ma'am—but none of our lifts go that way!"

"No, darling—he's not a <u>ski</u> bum. He's a <u>bum</u> bum."

"*I'm worried about Junior. His skis came back without him!*"

"Edna! Will you stop humming 'The Impossible Dream' when I'm trying to concentrate!"

Ski Courtesy Tip Number 25
Skiers should not stop where they will obstruct a trail,
or where they will not be visible from above.

". . . Thinks the world of his new skis."

"Dave's the living proof of reincarnation.
No one could be as clumsy as he is in one lifetime!"

"*Now this pair was owned by a little old lady with acrophobia.*"

"How long did they say we'd be stuck?"

Ski Safety Tip Number 10
It is better to go out overdressed than underdressed.

"Yes, sir, when they made him, they broke the mould!"

"Could you keep your eyes peeled for a set of lost car keys?"

Ski Safety Tip Number 21
Before doing anything unpredictable, first glance behind you.

*"No, today I want you to teach my friend.
I learned yesterday."*

Ski Courtesy Tip Number 23
When overtaking another skier, a suitable shout is a courteous warning.

"What happened after I waved to all my fans out there in television land?"

"But it looks so easy on television."

"May I make a suggestion?"

"Harold marches to the beat of a different drummer."

"First and foremost, Mr. Philman, you must learn to relax."

"Bear in mind that my ski boots probably weigh thirty pounds."

Cross Country Survival Tip Number 9
In the event of a sudden storm, seek shelter and conserve energy.

"About these ski brakes—are they drum or disc?"

"Nonsense, Marge—
it's never too windy for skiing."

"What's that? Another new ski gadget?"

"They say he's the most fearless skier on the mountain."

"Lionel! You come down here this instant!!"

"First, let's master walking — then we'll consider learning aerials."

"I suppose we should exchange licences?"

*"Mirror, mirror, on the wall . . .
who's the best dressed skier of them all?"*

"This may sound silly,
but I'm beginning to miss the noise, crowds, traffic and smog."

"Then it's agreed, doctors . . .
the ski boot will have to come off."

"I'll bet Ingemar Stenmark doesn't have to make his own breakfast!"

"If the skiing is so fantastic, how come we can still get reservations?"

"Certainly, what kind of favour?"

"Beats the hell out of any ski lock!"

"Being of sound mind and body, I spent every last bit of my money on wine, women and skiing!"